Silk
FLOWERS

Silk FLOWERS

Complete color and style guide
for the creative crafter

Judith Blacklock

Chilton Book Company
Radnor, Pennsylvania

A QUARTO BOOK

Copyright © 1995 Quarto Inc.

ISBN 0–8019–8649–4

A CIP record for this book is
available from the Library of
Congress

This book was designed and
produced by
Quarto Inc.
The Old Brewery
6 Blundell Street
London N7 9BH

Senior art editor Julie Francis
Designer Vicki James
Photographer Paul Forrester
Prop buyer Jo Carlill
Senior editor Sally MacEachern
Editor Eileen Cadman
Picture research manager
Giulia Hetherington
Art director Moira Clinch
Editorial director Sophie Collins

Typeset in Great Britain by
Central Southern Typesetters
Manufactured by Regent
Publishing Services Ltd,
Hong Kong
Printed in China by
Leefung-Asco Printers Ltd.

Publisher's Note
The author and publishers have
made every effort to ensure that all
instructions given in this book are
safe and accurate, but they cannot
accept liability for any resulting
injury, loss or damage to either
property or person whether direct
or consequential and howsoever
arising. They would like to draw
particular attention to the following:
    Several of the arrangements in
this book include candles. It is
advisable to spray the arrangement
with flame retardant and to make
sure that flowers and foliage are
well clear of the candles. Never
leave lit candles unattended.
    Small berries and fruits should
be firmly glued into position and
kept out of reach of small children.
    Do not touch your eyes after
handling dry foam as it is an irritant.

CONTENTS

INTRODUCTION

INTRODUCTION

Over the past few years the technology of synthetic materials has improved and developed enormously, and today many artificial flowers are extremely beautiful. Some imitate nature to perfection, while others are just a joyous expression of color, texture, and form without any claims to realism. In addition to being beautiful, decorative, and botanically correct, artificial flowers are extremely easy to use. Many people fear that making even one arrangement will be expensive, but you will find that once this initial purchase is made it will prove its worth again and again.

Artificial flowers are permanent additions to your scheme of decoration and so can be regarded as a long-term investment in the same way as pictures or rugs. Most of the materials used retain their color for many years unless exposed to strong sunlight. This lasting quality makes it tempting to keep the same design unaltered, but part of the fun of doing your own arrangements is that they can be changed at will to link with the seasons or a change in decor. Once you start arranging artificial flowers, you will probably find that you want to change them around simply for the pleasure of working with such easy material and obtaining such decorative and pleasing results.

There are other advantages of using artificial plant material. The stems of artificial flowers can be eased into just about any position within the arrangement and there they will stay. This is not always possible with fresh flowers. The stems, made of flexible wire or wires covered with stem tape, plastic or latex, can be easily shortened and lengthened to fit different designs. They can also be manipulated to curve gently over the rim of a container, or placed to give movement and flow within the design, as well as hiding the mechanics.

For many people, spare time is now at a

premium, and artificial flowers require less maintenance than their fresh and dried counterparts. There is no need to give essential conditioning treatment to make them last longer; many can be dipped into a weak solution of liquid detergent and water, sprayed with a commercially available product to dispel the dust and help resist further buildup, or simply shaken.

Unlike fresh flowers, which must not be placed on televisions, in a draft, or near a radiator, artificial flowers can be placed anywhere. There is no need to keep topping up the water, spraying, or dead-heading – artificial flowers are virtually maintenance-free and central heating poses no threat.

Artificial flowers are a boon to the millions who suffer from hayfever or allergies, as they do not have pollen and consequently do not attract insects.

There is minimal mess when arranging artificial flowers – something which must gladden the heart of everyone who has ever created dried flower arrangements! In addition, they can be packed in boxes and stored under beds, under stairs, in cupboards, or in the attic, just about anywhere (although obviously too much damp should be avoided). It does not matter if you squash the flowers and leaves – they can be brought back to life easily by holding them over a boiling pan of water for a few seconds.

Artificial flowers can be mixed with fresh foliage to give a stunning display. Churches, conferences, and temples are beginning to realize the monetary advantage of having a stock of artificial flowers that they can add to the basic outline of an arrangement established with natural foliage. Look at the example on pages 86–9. This mantelpiece design was achieved by adding silk arum lilies and thistles to a framework of fresh foliage.

Mixing artificial and fresh flowers can widen the choice, especially when flowers are needed out of season. A friend or relative may yearn for bachelor's buttons for their wedding, but if that wedding is to be in winter when blue flowers generally are difficult to obtain, then an accent of a few silk bachelor's buttons added to a bouquet of fresh foliage and flowers can solve the problem. For that special day, a corsage may be required to match an outfit. Once again, the use of artificial flowers, either on their own or mixed with fresh or dried, may be just the answer.

Judith Blacklock

$\mathscr{S}$ILK $\mathscr{F}$LOWERS

THE COUNTLESS VARIETIES of artificial flowers available means that it can be difficult to make a cohesive selection. Pages 8–13 provide an overview of the points to bear in mind when making your choice.

FLOWER SELECTION

When selecting flowers and other plant material, bear the following points in mind:

It is always a good idea to invest in a certain number of blooms and to buy three, five, or more stems of a single variety, for example, five stems of daisies, five freesias, three daffodils. Buying mixed bunches with only a single example of each flower can be restrictive.

You could buy flowers with a close color harmony, for example, delphiniums, bachelor's buttons, and scabious, or which have the same season, for example, snowdrops, crocus, and daffodils.

If you are buying wild or country flowers, think twice about mixing them with more exotic flowers such as orchids.

A "pick" is the word given to a short, single stem supporting a spray of flowers, fruit, berries or foliage, or to a single heavier item such as a cabbage or fruit. Flowering picks are often a successful and cost-effective purchase since they usually bear flowers and buds in various stages of development. This gives a very naturalistic appearance, sometimes more difficult to achieve when you buy stems bearing single flowers all of one shape and size. These secondary stems can easily be cut from the main stem.

Novelty flowers, which are frequently used to enhance items such as boxes, gifts, etc., are more inexpensive. They are often excellent value for money, but check that the dyes are color-fast, especially if they are to be used in bridal work.

More expensive flowers are priced according to the amount of

work involved in their design and production, where they are manufactured, the quality of the dyes used, the price of the raw materials, and the amount of hand work rather than machine work involved. Usually the more expensive a flower is, the more real it will appear. Often you will get the quality you pay for. Observing the leaves is often a good guide to quality. The color should be as close to reality as possible. Sometimes good-quality leaves have a double thickness, with the back covering the wire leaf spine. The backing is often of a slightly different hue to increase the realism.

SILK FLOWERS

Pure silk flowers are exceptionally beautiful. Because of their cost, they are less readily available than polyester blends, but they are still used extensively in the millinery trade.

The most widely seen artificial flowers are made of polyester blends. Often referred to as silk flowers (as they are in this book), they are much less expensive than pure silk and are easy to care for. Many are extremely realistic, so much so that it is difficult to distinguish them from their fresh counterparts. The vast majority of the flowers shown in this book are made from polyester blends.

DRIED-LOOK FLOWERS

A different finishing process produces flowers that imitate dried rather than fresh flowers. These "dried-look" flowers usually have more muted colors; the petals and leaves have a crinkly margin and feel slightly crisp to the touch; and the leaf color tends to be gray-green rather than a more vibrant "living" green. Dried-look artificial flowers have a strong affinity to dried flowers, and they look marvelous used together, when the size and stronger color of the artificial flowers gives substance and interest to the arrangement.

You can mix both types of silk flower in a large arrangement, but for a small design it is generally better to choose one or the other to give a more cohesive effect.

The vast majority of silk flowers are easy to care for. Many can be dipped in a gentle solution of soap, such as liquid detergent and water, shaken and either hung up to dry or rearranged. Some manufacturers simply recommend shaking them at regular intervals. There are several sprays on the market which magically dispel the dust quickly and effectively. Alternatively you can use a hair dryer on a gentle heat to blow the flowers or use a paintbrush to remove the dust from volumetric flower heads such as daffodils.

The silk flowers shown on these pages hint at the glorious array of colors and shapes available in pure silk (top left), dried-look (top right), and polyester blends (bottom).

OTHER FLOWERS

ALTHOUGH SILK and polyester-blend flowers are the most popular choice, artificial flowers are also crafted from a number of other materials. Each type varies in appearance and texture and can be mixed with silk flowers or used alone in arrangements.

COTTON FLOWERS

Cotton flowers are exceptionally beautiful, and the leaves are extremely realistic with good gradations of color. The pedestal arrangement on pages 92–3 contains a large number of cotton flowers.

They should be cared for by gentle shaking and then using a paintbrush to remove any dust that has settled in crevices.

PARCHMENT FLOWERS

Parchment flowers are created from natural fibers matted onto paper sheets which are then dried and bleached in the sun. They are hand painted and finally twisted and shaped. Occasionally the wire forming the spine of the leaves comes away from the parchment, but it can simply be cut off. You can change the color of parchment flowers by painting them with diluted watercolor paint. They have been added to the arrangements on pages 92–3 and 80–1. A soft paintbrush or hair dryer will remove any accumulated dust, and they can be gently shaken at regular intervals.

PAPER FLOWERS

The majority of paper flowers are simple and inexpensive. They look most effective in small arrangements and when added to wreaths, swags and garlands. They have been added to the arrangement on pages 76–7.

LATEX FLOWERS

The surface of flowers, berries, fruits, and foliage which have been dipped in latex bear a light coating of a whitish residue which is most attractive. Latex flowers and vegetables are used for the arrangements on pages 38–41, 62–3, and 96–7. Care for latex flowers is the same as for cotton.

RUBBER FLOWERS

Artificial plant material made from rubber is particularly effective when the flowers it is imitating have a waxy texture and bold form. The anthuriums used on pages 90–1 are a good example. Rubber can be washed in hot soapy water.

Flowers can be crafted from a variety of materials, such as cotton (left), parchment (middle top), paper (middle bottom), latex (right top), and rubber (right bottom).

FRUIT, VEGETABLES, AND FOLIAGE

MANUFACTURERS HAVE made great strides in producing realistic artificial foliage, fruits, and vegetables. Mixing artificial fruit and vegetables with silk flowers provides exciting contrasts in form and texture.

FRUITS AND BERRIES

Fruits and berries are frequently sold on a stem. The size of the stem varies according to cost. In larger-scale flower arrangements, the whole spray of plums may be used in order to be in scale with the flowers. In smaller designs, swags, and wreaths, it is better to cut the fruits off the stem, retaining only a short secondary stem (see pages 44–5). When cutting a stem of fruits or vegetables into smaller parts, only the stem should be discarded. The leaves will always come in handy. Never throw away a leaf! If you have fruits that are

unwired, try placing a drop of hot molten glue at the base of the fruit. A wire can often be run smoothly into the fruit at this point as the glue will have melted the tough outer coating.

VEGETABLES

Artificial vegetables are made from silk, polyester, plastic, latex, and other materials. They can appear completely realistic or simply fun. Some are supplied complete with a pick (a short stem) so that it is easy to secure them in foam. Others can easily be attached to wire or sticks with a dab of glue from a glue gun.

FOLIAGE

When choosing leaves, look for those with a good color which are not too shiny. Many flowers have a profuse amount of foliage on the stem so there is not always the need to add extra foliage.

Variegated foliage is foliage of more than one color. Buy it with restraint until you are totally sure of your requirements, as it is the plain green counterpart that is generally the most useful purchase. A little variegation however can give an interesting accent of color.

Choose only one or two varieties

of foliage if you are using a wide variety of flowers. Conversely, if you are using only a single variety of flowers you can give added interest by using a greater variety of foliage.

If your designs are large, you may wish to use whole sprays of leaves, but when purchasing it is always useful to consider whether your spray can be cut down into smaller pieces. Garlands of foliage are often an excellent investment. Apart from using them in their own right, they can also be used to give bulk to more substantial garlands or to embellish topiary frameworks. They can be cut into shorter lengths and used in arrangements where the diversity of the different leaf sizes gives a most naturalistic appearance.

Foliage (right) is an essential ingredient of many arrangements, whereas vegetables (top), fruit, and berries (bottom) can be used on their own or to add variety to a flower arrangement.

CONTAINERS

A CONTAINER is an integral part of many artificial flower arrangements, and the wide variety available may make it hard to decide on the best one. A special container may provide inspiration, or a particular selection of colors will suggest a suitable vase or container.

SIZE

Consider whether the container is the right scale for the flowers you wish to use, and of the right material. It really comes down to common sense. If your container is small and made of glass or porcelain, you should choose flowers that are delicate, such as snowdrops, bluebells, or baby's breath, not, for example, the large hydrangea or the bold gerbera. Conversely, if your vase is large and strong, you will go for robust flowers with strong, large forms such as lilies and delphiniums.

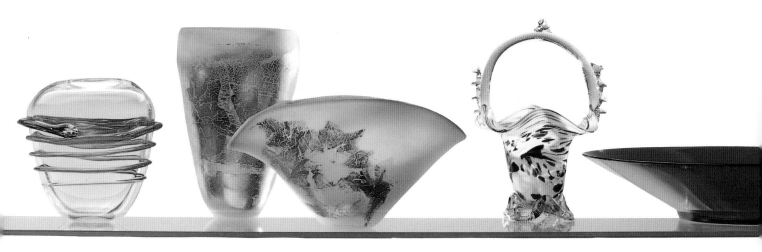

SHAPE AND PROPORTION

Choose shapes that are easiest to use for good effect – vases where it is difficult to go wrong. A symmetrically shaped container, such as the one center right, is frequently easier to use than one that is asymmetrically balanced, such as a pitcher or cornucopia.

In fresh and dried flower work, unless you have softly flowing plant material such as bear grass, a container with an incurving lip can be hard to use successfully. With silk flowers, because of the flexibility of their stems, just about any container can be put to good effect. However, whatever its shape, you need to consider relative proportions. The volume of the plant material should be approximately one and a half times that of the container. Alternatively arrange the plant material so it is one and a half times the height or width of the container, whichever is the greater.

DESIGN

Plain, unpatterned containers are relatively safe. If you have a multi-colored container, choose two or three of the colors for your flowers so that the design will enhance the container but not overpower it. If your container is white and shiny, use some white or pale pastel flowers so that there is a harmonious link between container and flowers. If you use only dark colors in a white container or only light colors in a dark container, there will be too strong a division between the elements of the design (unless you desire this particular effect).

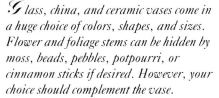

Glass, china, and ceramic vases come in a huge choice of colors, shapes, and sizes. Flower and foliage stems can be hidden by moss, beads, pebbles, potpourri, or cinnamon sticks if desired. However, your choice should complement the vase.

MATERIAL

One of the many beauties of
artificial flowers is that the
container does not have to be
waterproof. Terracotta, for
example, is a porous material and
care is needed when using water-
retentive foam, but with artificial
flowers there is no such problem.
Papier-mâché is another attractive
porous material which is ideal for
colorful containers.

Another advantage of artificial
flowers is that the container does
not have to be perfect. Vases are
often heavily discounted for having
a chip – and this is frequently on
the rim. It is very satisfying to
angle an artificial stem artfully
over the chip to give the
impression of a perfect vase.

Antique containers look lovely
with flowers – pottery jugs,
Victorian handbasins, copper urns,
brass bowls – and here again the

less-than-perfect specimen can be
brought into play instead of lying
forlornly on a kitchen shelf. With a
glass container, stems or foam can
easily be disguised with moss,
pebbles, potpourri, or even pasta.
If the container is of a visually
heavy material, such as stoneware,
cement or terracotta, it will need
more flowers than one made of
glass or china.

TRANSFORMING CONTAINERS

Containers for artificial flowers do
not have to be expensive. Even
plastic pots can be made to look
exciting.

Cut silk, burlap, or any other
attractive fabric into a circular
shape. Place the container on the

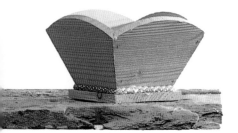

fabric and bring the raw edges up so they can be tucked or glued into the well of the container. Alternatively, give the fabric an adhesive backing by ironing on a specialist bonding product.

Stick double-sided tape around a container and then press silk leaves onto the tape. You can use this method to add twigs, moss, lichen, pressed leaves, cinnamon sticks, shells, or dried flowers to the outside of a container. A binding of raffia, ribbon, twine, or braid will help to keep the decoration in place.

Containers can be spray painted different colors, sponged with several colors (see the green and gold containers below), or marbled, using a craft kit.

WREATHS, SWAGS, AND GARLANDS

You can buy wreath bases in a variety of materials from foam to twisted vines; you can also make your own using a wire frame base (bought or made yourself), twigs, vines, or plant material with strong stems, such as clematis.

Swag cage frames filled with foam are an easy option for making swags and garlands. However, you can improvise with foam rectangles and a length of thin plastic. The plastic film from a drycleaner or laundry is ideal. Place a foam rectangle on the plastic film, wrap it around the foam, and tie a knot at each end. Continue placing foam rectangles, wrapping and knotting until you reach the desired length.

Freed from the need to use waterproof containers, silk flower arrangers can employ anything from baskets and clay pots to a pewter jug or a brass cartridge case.

$\mathscr{A}$CCESSORIES

SILK FLOWERS provide a marvelous opportunity for being adventurous: you can mix them with fresh foliage or dried flowers; you can disguise stems and mechanics with moss; you can add dried fruit slices, mushrooms, and shells for textural variety – you are limited only by your imagination.

FRESH FOLIAGE

When using fresh foliage, consider its life expectancy. Leaves that wilt quickly will spoil the effect. Generally speaking, evergreen shrubs will last longer, particularly those with waxy, glossy, or spiny leaves. Always give foliage from the yard or countryside a long drink of water before arranging, and cut the stem ends on a slant if they have been out of water for any length of time whatsoever.

Suitable foliage could include camellia, boxwood, laurel, myrtle, holly, and blue spruce. Eucalyptus, with its graceful stems, gives movement and flow to a design and will dry *in situ* and still remain attractive. Use long-lasting fresh foliage with artificial nasturtiums, iris, morning glory, daffodils, buttercups, or sweet peas. Longer-lasting flowers such as chrysanthemums, mature hydrangeas, poinsettias, orchids, or anthuriums can be mixed with artificial foliage when fresh foliage is difficult to obtain.

When placing artificial flowers in water, and to a lesser extent wet foam, be aware that if the stem has been covered in tape it may unravel. This is not really a

problem as the stems can easily be
retaped. Alternatively you can
keep the stems dry by placing the
stems of the artificial flowers in a
separate container within the
design or by coating the stem ends
with clear nail polish.

DRIED FLOWERS

Dried flowers diminish greatly in
volume as a result of the
dehydration process. Adding
dried-look silk flowers can give
instant impact, and few will be
aware that you have mixed dried
with artificial. For example, a few
dried-look silk sunflowers, by
virtue of their form, can give a
strong focus of interest to a
selection of dried flowers.

MOSS

There are several different types of
moss widely available, and all give
an exciting extra dimension to
work with fresh, dried, or artificial
flowers. Great care must be
exerted when taking fresh and
dried moss from the wild – check
first whether there are any
restrictions in your area.

Sphagnum moss is inexpensive
and available from most florists. It
is usually purchased fresh, when it
is an attractive green color. Even
though it dries to a less attractive

brown-green, it is still useful for
quickly covering large expanses of
foam. Flower and foliage stems
easily penetrate the moss, which
will reduce the need to keep
adding stems in order to hide every
bit of foam. Place the moss on the
foam while it is still slightly damp
when it is easier to use. Secure
with hairpins of wire or moss pins.
Any unused moss can be stored for
several months in a cool place in a
dark plastic bag.

Soft and springy when fresh,
reindeer moss (also known as
lichen moss) becomes brittle when
dry. However, commercially
available moss has usually been
treated with a glycerin solution so
that it remains permanently soft –
rather like a sponge. It is flexible
and easy to use, and combines
beautifully with artificial flowers
and fruits, giving a pleasing
textural contrast. It is often dyed
in a range of colors. Although the
stronger colors such as red may be
used to give color accent to a
design, green and other natural
colors are more useful. Reindeer

*Accessories shown on these pages include
(clockwise from top left): fresh foliage,
moss, potpourri, cereals, dried flowers,
and seedpods.*

moss is often sold in cellophane packets and expands to fill the space, so check the weight of the moss before buying. When used in swags, garlands, and wreaths, it can cover a large area relatively inexpensively.

Tillandsia moss is in fact an air plant – *Tillandsia usenoides*. In its natural state, it is soft gray and has a lovely crinkly texture, but when sold for dried and artificial flower work, it has often been dyed green. More unruly than reindeer moss, it gives a light, natural, untamed effect. It has been used to fill in between the fruits and flowers in the crate design on pages 100–1. A brilliant alternative "tillandsia moss" which has been created from wood pulp is now available.

SHELLS

The wreath on pages 42–3 uses shells to give another form and texture. Great care must be taken that any shells used in flower design are commonly available – preferably beach-collected.

MUSHROOMS

There are many different artificial and dried mushrooms which can be used, but the most widely available are sponge mushrooms and golden mushrooms.

There are two attractive sides to the sponge mushroom. One side is smooth and the other ridged. Depending on which texture you wish to show, you can attach a small toothpick to the opposite side with strong glue. The toothpick can then easily be inserted into your foam or moss. The design on pages 66–7 has used sponge mushrooms.

Golden mushrooms are used in the design on pages 48–9. They look like carved wooden pieces and have a smooth texture and short stalks. Sometimes these stalks are long enough to insert securely in foam, but if they are too short, they can easily be extended with a wire and a drop of glue.

FRAGRANCES

If you find fragrance lacking in your designs, spray them with one of the extensive choice of floral sprays now available. Just follow the instructions on the spray. Usually a couple of puffs is all you need to give a lingering perfume. To choose an appropriate spray, use one that matches your design. For example, an arrangement using blue spruce and fir cones would suit a pine-scented spray. An arrangement of roses and lavender would suit a romantic mix which included these two flowers.

Alternatively, place a dish

containing potpourri near the arrangement, or hide the foam by covering it with a potpourri mixture (in the same way cinnamon sticks hide the foam on pages 76–7).

Wood absorbs fragrant oils very easily, and carved woods impregnated with oil are delightful when placed in the same room as a flower arrangement.

Some artificial flowers may be purchased with the petals impregnated with a fragrance. Squeezing the petals gently between the fingers will fill the room with the scent. If you mix some fresh blue spruce or eucalyptus with your flowers, you will obtain a natural fragrance.

RIBBON AND FABRIC

There is a wide array of ribbon available – patterned, plain, and wired. Wired ribbon lends itself particularly well to work with swags, garlands, and wreaths.

Ribbon is an excellent means of covering foam quickly and inexpensively and giving contrasting textural interest. There are many complicated methods of producing bows, but some of the most effective are very simple to produce (see page 25).

Paper ribbon comes tightly rolled and can take ages to unwind. Dampen your hands first.

FRUIT SLICES

Dried fruit slices can be purchased ready packaged and are a delightful addition to wreaths, swags, and garlands. They can easily be prepared at home. Thin-skinned fruit such as lemons, grapefruits, and oranges should be sliced thinly and then placed on paper towels to absorb any juice. Place the slices on fresh absorbent paper on baking trays and heat in a slow oven for several hours, turning occasionally. Reduce the heat if they start to brown. Orange slices have been used on pages 44–5.

CANDLES

Candles add a festive touch to arrangements for special occasions (see pages 86–7) and a note of elegance to a simple arrangement such as Rising High on pages 98–9. However, always remember that candles can be dangerous, particularly when using artificial rather than real plant material. Never leave lighted candles unattended.

Accessories shown on these pages include (clockwise from top left): candles, fabric, moss and paper ribbons, twig bundles, oil-impregnated wood, potpourri, sponge and golden mushrooms, dried fruit slices, lotus seed heads, cinnamon sticks, and shells.

EQUIPMENT

THE ONLY vital pieces of equipment are floral foam, wire cutters, wires, and stem tape. The other items mentioned here are useful but not essential.

FOAM

Floral foam is a boon to arrangers of fresh, dried, and artificial flowers. Green foam is usually used for fresh flowers. Soak it in water for a couple of minutes to give the flowers a source of water. Gray foam, used with dried and artificial flowers, does not absorb water. Rectangular blocks of foam are the most common shape, but spheres, circles, cones, and cylinders are also available. When handling dry foam, take care not to touch your eyes, because it is a very harsh irritant.

WIRE CUTTERS

To cut the thinner stems of artificial flowers, buy a good pair of snips or florists' scissors. A pair of wire cutters or pliers is essential for the thicker, heavier ones. Electrical wire cutters are easy to use but expensive. Try out a few cutters and choose a pair that feels comfortable to hold and is capable of cutting wires up to ⅜ inch thick.

WIRES

Wires can be purchased in various weights and lengths. For the work in this book you will need heavy-gauge, medium-gauge, and light-gauge wires. Buy the longest available, particularly for heavy-gauge. When working with heavier material, ask for 1.25 mm or 1.00 mm (18 g or 19 g) wires; for general work 0.90 mm or 0.71 mm (20 g or 22 g) wires; and for light work 0.56 mm or 0.46 mm (24 g or 26 g).

STEM TAPE

Stem tape is also known as gutta percha. It is principally used in silk flower work for covering wires so that they are as unobtrusive as

possible. It is sold on reels and is not expensive. Several colors are available, but the most useful is one of the many shades of green.

GLUE AND GLUE GUNS

A glue gun is a boon to any work with artificial flowers. Low-temperature glue guns are popular since there is less chance of minor burns if glue drips onto the skin. However, glue from a hot gun usually dries clearer. Check that you buy the correct glue sticks for the gun. Avoid purchasing an inexpensive disposable glue gun. Use strong-bonding liquid glue until you can afford to buy a better one.

CANDLECUPS

Candlecups, made of metal or plastic, are for placing in containers with a small opening. Candlecups have a protrusion which can easily be inserted into the narrow opening. For security use some floral fixative around the protrusion. Candlecups are usually black, white or bronze. They are less conspicuous if they are sprayed to match the candlestick.

FLORAL CLAY

This is a sticky substance ideal for joining the base of a frog to a container or candlecup. Surfaces must be clean and dry. Floral clay needs to be kneaded a little before use. Its adhesive powers work best if your hands are warm.

FROG

A frog is a pronged disk obtainable in plastic or metal in two sizes, a smaller one for general use and a larger one for bigger designs. If you are using a lot of heavy material, invest in a metal frog with six pins as it will support a greater weight.

FLORISTS' TAPE

Florists' tape should not be confused with stem tape. Florists' tape is a strong adhesive tape that sticks firmly to floral foam, unlike clear tape.

CHICKEN WIRE

Also known as wire netting, it is used to give extra support to stems.

Equipment shown on these pages includes: (top from left to right) floral foam in a variety of shapes, foam-filled pot, bouquet holder and swag cases; (bottom from left to right) glue gun, wire cutters, pliers, moss pins, stem tape, frogs and floral clay, florists' tape, candle holder, candlecup, toothpicks, reels of wire, light, medium and heavy gauge wires, chicken wire, and plastic dish.

*T*ECHNIQUES

THERE ARE some basic techniques that are specific to working with artificial flowers, foliage, fruit and vegetables, and others that are shared with fresh flower arranging. All of them are simple and easy to do.

CHAMFERING FOAM

Use a sharp knife to remove sharp angles. This increases the surface area.

In fresh flower work, a foam block has to be cut so that it rises above the rim of the container or vase to allow stems to be angled downward over the rim of the container. However, as the wires in artificial flower stems can easily be bent to curve over the sides of the vase, the foam does not need to rise above the level of the container unless a greater surface area is needed for inserting stems (usually the case when you have a tall vase with a narrow opening).

CUTTING WIRE

A wire (or wires) runs through the center of most artificial flowers and foliage stems to give them support and flexibility. If the wire is covered with a layer of rubber, plastic, or latex, cut through this with scissors and then attack the wire itself with wire cutters or pliers.

STEM TAPING

1 To practice, use a single thick wire. Take a piece of stem tape about 6 inches long. Hold one end tightly on the tip of the wire. With the other hand, wind the free end once or twice around the wire tip, pulling it slightly.

2 Twirl the wire with one hand, holding the loose end of the tape taut with the other hand. The tape should neatly overlap itself around the wire.

3 To finish, twist the tape onto itself so that it will not unwrap and tear off any remaining tape. After a little practice, you can adapt this method to suit individual stems. It is thrilling to master the technique and be able to cover the wire or stem in seconds.

LENGTHENING STEMS

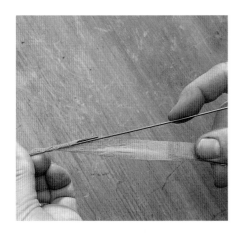

1 Wrap stem tape down the stem you wish to lengthen to the point where it will overlap the second wire. Select a wire that is the right weight and length to support the size and weight of your stem. Place this extension wire alongside the stem wire.

2 Stem-tape the two wires together. For extra security, you can add a touch of glue at the join before using the stem tape.

LENGTHENING STEMS – SINGLE LEG MOUNT

1 Use a single leg mount for light stems. Bend a length of wire so that one end is longer than the other. Place it along the stem so that the shorter end of the wire is the same length as the stem end. Wrap the longer end of wire tightly around both the stem and the shorter end until both ends are the same length.

2 Use stem tape to disguise the joint and the wire.

LENGTHENING STEMS – DOUBLE LEG MOUNT

1 Use a double leg mount for heavier stems. Bend a length of wire so that one end is longer than the other. Place it alongside the stem so that the shorter end of the wire protrudes beyond the stem end. Wrap the longer end of wire tightly around both the stem and the shorter end.

2 Use stem tape to disguise the joint and the wire.

FALSE STEMS

1 If a stem is too weak to be inserted in foam, create a false stem. Thread a wire through the base of the leaves.

2 Twist the wire ends together. Cover with stem tape.

GLUING

A glue gun releases hot glue through the nozzle when you press the trigger. The molten glue bonds within seconds. Glue is invaluable for keeping heavy items in place in a swag or wreath, giving extra security when lengthening stems, decorating pots, and making wired ribbon.

SECURING FOAM

Use florist's tape to keep foam firmly in place while arranging flowers. Strap the tape from one side of the container to the other over the foam. Cut away any obtrusive ends when the arrangement is complete. Frogs and fix also help to keep foam in position.

SECURING STEMS

1 You can use 2-inch chicken wire instead of foam to keep flower stems in place. Take a piece of wire three times larger than the opening of your container. Scrunch it to fit, keeping the loose ends up so that they can be hooked around the stems to give extra security.

2 You can use chicken wire in conjunction with sand or a pinholder for extra security. Pass the tallest or heaviest stems through the netting and then between the pins of the pinholder, or into the sand to establish a framework.

Alternatively, ½-inch chicken wire can be placed over the foam and wired in place. If your stems are close to ½ inch thick, use 1-inch wire.

WIRING LOTUS SEEDHEADS

Take a wire through the seed head. Make a small hook at one end and pull the wire down until the hook is embedded in the seed head.

WIRING CINNAMON STICKS

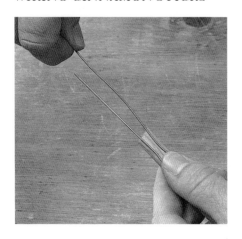

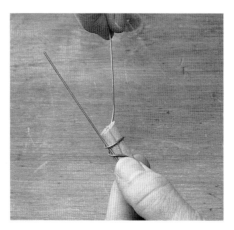

1 Bend a piece of wire into a loop so that one end is longer than the other. Hold the loop end against the cinnamon stick.

2 Wind the long end around the short end and the cinnamon stick until secure.

3 The ends can now be cut to the required length and inserted into foam.

WIRING MUSHROOMS

Place glue on the central base area of the mushroom. Press the end of a medium or strong gauge wire onto the glue.

WIRING FRUIT

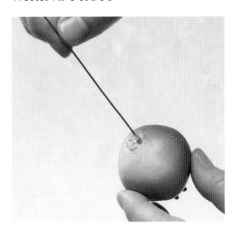

If fruit is not on a pick, glue a short wire to the base. Hold in position until the glue sets.

CANDLE LEGS

Forcing a candle into foam makes a large hole and the candle is relatively unstable. Instead, tape 3–5 toothpicks around the candle. Push them into the foam until the candle is resting on the surface.

RIBBON BOW

1 Take a length of ribbon and find the central point. Cross the ends over the center and hold firmly.

2 Wrap a length of wire tightly around the center of the bow. The protruding ends of the wire will be inserted into foam.

ORGANDY BOW

1 Make several loops in a length of organdy ribbon, leaving two free ends.

2 Twist a length of wire firmly around the loops and ends to keep them secure. The wire ends will be inserted into foam.

$\mathcal{C}$OLOR

$\mathcal{C}$OLOR IS one of the most exciting and fascinating aspects of design. Its emotive quality is considerable. Successful use of color is not just a question of flair and instinct. There are a few basic rules that can easily be learned to achieve the best results.

$\mathcal{B}$lues combined with neutral colors give an instant impression of coolness *that is very refreshing.*

If you find it difficult to choose flowers, think of your own color preferences, not just for flowers, but for any aspect of life. Some people prefer the warm colors associated with the sun – orange, yellow, and gold, or the colors associated with the landscape – blues and greens. Others may perhaps have one or two colors that dominate their wardrobe. You might have decorated your home with floral fabrics based on a pink theme or perhaps marbled and dragged effects in peach and terracotta. Look at your clothes, furnishings, and decor, and you may well find that you do have color preferences.

COLOR WHEEL

To learn more about color, it is important to understand the basic color wheel.

This is formed from primary and secondary colors. The primaries are red, blue, and yellow, which are the only colors that cannot be created by mixing other colors together. The secondary colors are orange, violet, and green, which are created by mixing two primary colors in equal amounts.

Generally, red, orange, and yellow are considered to be warm colors, although you can get warm and cool shades of red, for example, while green, blue, and purple are cool colors. Colors opposite each other, such as orange and blue, are known as complementaries, while any two colors next to each other (purple and red, or orange and yellow, for example) are known as adjacent.

Black, white, and gray are not shown on the color wheel because they are not part of the spectrum. Known as neutral colors, they can be included in any color scheme without changing it. In flower arranging terms, brown and green also acts as neutrals, since their addition has a harmonizing effect.

Generally speaking, harmonious designs are more difficult to compose without the restful addition of green – it is nature's harmonizer. Green is the color of fresh new growth, mature summer leaves, and the hardy evergreens of winter. It holds together all flower designs, whatever combination of colors are used. Add green to a monochromatic color scheme, and you will provide extra interest that will enhance rather than detract from your color statement.

$\mathcal{O}$range and yellow flowers arranged in terracotta pots give an impression of warmth *and vitality.*

*T*ints and shades *of blue form a virtually monochromatic design which harmonizes with neutral white, gray, and green.*

*B*lue and purple, and green and blue are adjacent *colors. Using them together produces a restful arrangement that is easy on the eye.*

A n arrangement using one color and type of flower is known as monochromatic. *The browns and greens act as neutral colors.*

*P*urples and yellows are complementary *colors which enhance each other. The green acts as a neutral background.*

29

Brown is the color of the earth, wood, bark, and autumn leaves. Brown is often at its most effective when used with the warm colors of the fall. It gives depth and contrast.

No single color scheme will appeal to everyone. However, if the information on these pages is borne in mind when selecting colors, you will have harmony in your design and a pleasing balance.

MONOCHROMATIC COLOR SCHEMES

A monochromatic color scheme uses only one color. Adhering strictly to such a color scheme, without the use of green or brown, would be highly restrictive. This category is rarely included in competitive show classes as it is too easy for the competitor to err and thus be disqualified.

The sunflower arrangement center left is the closest this book gets to a monochromatic arrangement. Although only one type and color of flower has been used and the effect is strongly yellow, the addition of green and brown adds a subtle touch of harmonizing color.

TINTS AND SHADES

Arrangements using one basic color in varying tints and shades are close to being monochromatic and rely heavily on the good use of texture and contrast. For example, in a blue design, choose light blue scabious, bright blue delphiniums, and dark blue pansies.

Another word for a tint is a pastel. A tint is achieved by adding white to a color: pink is a tint of red, lemon is a tint of yellow. If black is added to a color, it becomes darker and this is a shade. A shade of red is crimson, a shade of blue is navy. Tints and shades of just one color might seem restrictive, but even the same design can look different using different tonal colors.

ADJACENT COLOR SCHEMES

These are easy color schemes to work with and are useful when you are working to develop your own expertise with color. They are schemes that are easy to live with – calm and gentle without sharp contrasts. The easiest way to understand an adjacent color scheme is to look at the color wheel on page 29. Any two colors next to each other are adjacent.

COMPLEMENTARY COLOR SCHEMES

To understand this, look at the color wheel. Just as adjacent colors lie close to each other and have something in common, complementary colors lie opposite each other and have nothing in common. Red is the complementary color of green, orange of blue, and yellow of violet. When they are used together, you immediately get a vivid color scheme, each color making the other more intense. It is often more effective not to use two pure hues, but use a tint or shade of one, for this will be more restful on the eye. Using one of the two colors as an accent rather than in equal amounts always works well. Think of red berries shining among green holly leaves or orange nasturtiums against a blue sky.

These arrangements demonstrate (top) the use of tints, (center) a monochromatic color scheme, and (bottom) adjacent colors.

WARM AND COOL COLORS

Red and orange are warm colors; green and blue are cool colors. Violet and yellow can appear cool or warm according to the colors with which they are combined. It has been scientifically proved that people feel cooler more quickly in a room painted blue than they do in one painted orange. Similarly, the wreath of blue flowers and shells bottom right would give a pleasant refreshing effect during hot summer days. The fountain of flowers middle right and the swag on pages 48–9 would bring warmth and vitality into the home during the cold winter months.

COLOR AND CONTAINERS

Neutralized colors are those that are weak, as opposed to tints and shades which have had the pure color diluted by the addition of white or black. Examples would be beige, eau-de-nil, and soft gray. These undemanding colors are ideal for containers, since they do not compete but enhance. A container that is patterned can look stunning but can be harder to use effectively, and the stronger the pattern the harder it will be to create an overall design that is a harmonious whole. The result can be a divided design where the flowers form one part and the container the other, so care is needed to link the colors of the container with those of the flowers, perhaps picking out only two or three of the colors from the pattern.

LIGHTING

Good lighting will show off any flower arrangement to good effect. A strong natural light will always emphasize the light and shadow in flowers beautifully, but very often flowers have to be viewed in artificial light.

It is quite remarkable how pastel flowers show up well in a candlelit room and how blues and purples disappear. Large buildings such as churches and conference rooms are often dimly lit. In such rooms blue flowers tend to be lost, but the effect of pale yellow or peach flowers can be glorious.

Blue flowers, however, are radiant under fluorescent or strip lighting, but the combination of this blue-yellow light on red flowers is disastrous. It muddies or browns even the most vibrant reds. You may think that flowers are rarely lit by strip lighting but outside the home, strip lighting is much more prevalent – for example in offices, meeting rooms, schools, and churches.

Electric filament or tungsten lighting, with its warm yellow glow, enhances all colors in the warm half of the color wheel but is far less kind to blues, violets, and purples.

These arrangements show the use of (top) complementary colors, (center) warm colors, and (bottom) cool colors.

ᗪESIGN

IF YOU understand the principles behind good design, you will be able to re-create the arrangements in the project section with greater ease. You will also be able to create your own stunning designs that will impress your visitors and give much pleasure to yourself as well.

FORM

Flowers can be loosely divided into one of three groups, according to their form. When you turn to the project section of this book, you will see that in many of the designs the flowers and plant material are referred to by their forms – round, line, or spray. This is to enable you to create these designs according to the form of the flowers you may already possess, or to adapt the design to suit your personal preferences. Some designs need a mixture of all three forms; others are composed simply of flowers of a single form.

Round flowers have a strong and compelling form – hydrangeas, marigolds, and peonies all have this quality. In traditional designs they are usually placed in the central and lower area of the design to help achieve good balance.

Unlike round flowers, which have color interest only at the flowering tip, linear flowers have the flowering parts along the stem, which takes color deep into the arrangement. Examples are delphiniums, foxgloves, snap-dragons, and stocks. By virtue of their contrasting form, they complement round flowers.

Spray material, with its soft, flowing branches, creates a link between the round and linear flowers. Spray foliage is ideal for creating the initial framework in large traditional designs. Delicate spray flowers fill the design easily and give grace and movement. Examples are spray carnations, spray chrysanthemums, and gypsophila.

Once you have become accustomed to attributing form to different varieties of flowers, finding an effective combination becomes second nature.

In the pedestal arrangement (top), the linear flowers lead the eye into the design, the round flowers give strong focal interest, and the spray flowers link the two forms. (Bottom) The combination of opposite textures, ranging from the smooth, curved glass to the knobbly gourds, is extremely effective.

TEXTURE

Texture, when referring to plants and flowers, means how you imagine the surface will feel to the touch. An anthurium appears waxy and smooth, a thistle rough and prickly. Combining opposing textures enhances the qualities of each and is of particular importance in monochromatic color schemes. Contrasting texture can also be introduced by ribbon, candles, cinnamon sticks, moss, fruits and vegetables, and foliage. They can all enhance the beauty of the flowers.

BALANCE

Not only must your completed design not fall over, but it must not appear to be about to topple over. Place your largest flowers or most strongly colored plant material about two-thirds of the way down from the top of a traditional design and away from the sides. The exception, and of course there always is an exception, is in Dutch flower paintings, where the most important flower was placed at the very top. These were contrived masterpieces composed on paper by the artist; they never actually existed as "real" arrangements, although they can be recreated with your artificial plant material quite easily.

SCALE

Scale means the size of each of the elements in relation to every other. The scale of a snowdrop is small, that of a lily is large. Where there is too great a difference in size, there will be conflict rather than harmony. A berry on its own is too small to be effective, or even noticed, with the majority of plant material. However, if 20 or so are grouped on a stem, the scale is increased and it will look comfortable even if placed with the large-scale lilies, peonies, and

hydrangeas. A rule that seems to work is to avoid placing flowers with others that are more than twice their size unless you incorporate others of a transitional size, or sprays of smaller flowers or berries. These will allow the eye to flow smoothly from one to another.

PROPORTION

Proportion refers to amounts. This is most relevant to the relationship between the container and the flowers. Flowers with an overall volume one and a half times greater than the container will result in good proportions. In contemporary designs, and some traditional designs such as the decorated basket, it may be the container, not the flowers, that will be dominant. The same formula applies, but the container will be a more important feature than the flowers.

Proportion can also refer to height. An approximate rule of thumb is to place the flowers so that they are one and a half times the height or width of the container, whichever is the greater.

The heavy outer container (top) gives a stronger visual weight to the lower part of the design, providing stability and balance. (Center) The delicate flowers were chosen to harmonize with the scale of the basket. (Bottom) The dense mass of flowers is approximately one and a half times that of the container, forming a well-proportioned arrangement.

CONTRAST

Where there are only subtle color contrasts, perhaps most noticeable in monochromatic designs with mixed flowers, it is important to have contrast of tints and shades within that color range. Textural contrasts are also vital – the more limited the color range, the more important it is to have strong textural contrasts to bring life and interest to the overall design. There is a great range of textures in artificial flower design, but one of the most important combinations is a smooth texture contrasting with the more intricate texture of the majority of flowers. Without it a design can look cluttered and fussy, devoid of flair and style.

DOMINANCE

Designs which give equal importance to the colors or forms can seem uneasy. The eye and the mind seem to feel more comfortable if one component in a design dominates and takes control. This can be put to good effect practically by allowing one tint or shade to dominate, one particular flower to dominate, or one particular texture to dominate. In the same way, either the container or the flowers should be more important. The style of design usually dictates your choice.

RHYTHM

In flower arranging parlance, rhythm means movement or flow within the design. Rhythm gives more interest – the eye moves from one part to another and back again. Movement can be built up in a design by various means. It can be created by repetition of form and color through the design so that the eye can move smoothly from one element to another by virtue of a connecting feature. Radiating stems from a central area also helps to build up sympathetic movement.

The smooth apples, springy moss, and light paper ribbon (top) form interesting contrasts in shape and texture, while the orange slices and twisting willow give depth and movement. (Center) Foliage, in varying forms, tints, and tones, creates a dense framework, but it is the roses, with their strong form and color, that dominate. (Bottom) Movement is created by the radiation of the stems from the central area, by the placement of the dominant white lilies through the design, and by the line of artichokes and thistles which echoes that of the lilies.

GETTING STARTED

SILK FLOWERS are a pleasure to work with, create minimal mess, and will last for years. Enjoy yourself.

It is important to read through the initial pages of this book, particularly if you are completely new to flower arranging. You will feel more confident if you have some idea of the variety of materials available and have grasped some of the basic principles of color and design.

There are only a few simple techniques to learn. Refer back to pages 24–7 whenever you need to refresh your memory, or if you come across a new technique during the course of a project.

You do not need a large amount of space for flower arranging, but it is important to have a clear working surface – perhaps a table or kitchen counter – and good lighting.

The projects are designed so that you can either follow them exactly, or adapt them to suit the flowers and containers you have available. Although specific flowers are mentioned in most arrangements, it is always possible to substitute other suitable round, spray, or linear flowers.

ARRANGING TIPS

❀ When you purchase your plant material, the flower heads and leaves may well have been flattened or squashed. It is amazing how much life you can instill into them with a little manipulation. This is easily done by following a few simple points: If the leaves are positioned at different angles on the stem, make sure that the leaves are not all facing stiffly in the same direction but turning in the direction nature intended; give movement to leaves by easing the wire spine of the leaf into an arch; if the leaves have a dominant spine, turn them so that the spines are facing away from the viewer.

❀ Never throw away a leaf of any description if storage permits!

❀ The shape of latex, parchment, and some polyester-blend flowers can be altered. Take advantage of this quality and manipulate each flower to give a slightly different form.

❀ Do not cut stems unless necessary, since this may restrict opportunities for reuse. For many designs you can simply bend the bottom of the stems up. To insert these stems into foam, join the doubled stems together with wire or tape so that they can be inserted more securely and neatly.

❀ Picks of flowers bearing flowers and buds in different stages of development give a realistic group of flowers. Several picks of the same variety of flower can be used to create a pleasing arrangement.

❀ Use the minimum amount of foam that will support your stems securely.

❀ In a large design, any combination of flower material – silk, parchment, and latex, for example – can be used together successfully. In a smaller design, it is safer to work with just one medium.

❀ Any color combination will work together with a sufficient amount of green or brown, as these colors act as harmonizers.

❀ A rough guide to good proportion: think of one and a half times the volume of flowers and foliage to that of the container.

❀ To achieve good scale in your arrangement avoid using individual flowers that are more than twice as large as those closest to them in size.

❀ Position green foliage – fresh or artificial – first when it is an important part of your arrangement. This will establish the overall shape of the design before you start to add the flowers.

WREATHS, SWAGS, AND GARLANDS

*ALWAYS FESTIVE, wreaths, swags, and
garlands are fun to make because you can
experiment with all kinds of additional
materials, from dried orange slices and shells
to candles and ribbon. A glue gun will be
useful, as will ready-made wreath bases of
florist's foam, cage frames, and stub wires.
Wreaths and swags make attractive
centerpieces for tables, in addition to looking
decorative on walls and doors, while
garlands can be entwined around banisters,
trailed around a fireplace, or festooned
around a festive table.*

GARLAND OF ROSES

A SWIRLING garland of roses and grapevine entwined with a flourish of fabric would enhance a staircase, pillar, doorway, or fireplace whatever the occasion, whatever the time of year.

You will need:

1½ blocks of dry foam

18 swag cages, this will produce a 9-foot garland

medium or heavy gauge stub wires

a length of material, approximately twice as long as the linked cages and 5–6inches wide

grapevine garlands, the combined length to be approximately twice as long as the linked cages

10–12 large single pink latex roses

about 7 sprays cream latex roses

about 7 sprays pink latex roses

8–10 sprays cream latex dogwood

cream variegated foliage to complete

1 Cut each foam block into 18 equal-size rectangles: these will fill the cages exactly. Fill each cage and link them together. If you want a longer garland, add more cages. With stub wire, create a hanging loop at each side of the garland.

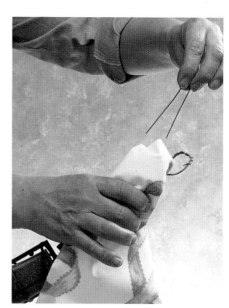

2 Take one end of the fabric and turn under the raw edges. Bend a stub wire to form a hairpin and secure the fabric to the foam.

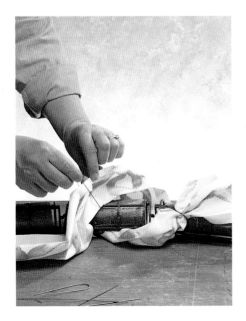

3 Wrap the fabric round and round the cages *very loosely* so there is plenty of space between the fabric and the cages. Secure at intervals with stub wire pins.

4 Cut the grapevine garlands into shorter lengths about 18 inches long. Wrap loosely around the cages and fabric, inserting the free ends into the foam. Secure with stub wire pins.

5 Place the large single roses at approximately the same intervals in a gentle, uneven wave along the garland. Do not place any too close to either end.

6 Place the cream spray roses in the garland.

7 Add the pink spray roses, remembering to work all around the garland and not just at the front. Run the cream dogwood in groups of twos and threes through the garland.

8 Cut the variegated foliage into smaller pieces and fill in to make the garland full and luxuriant when viewed from any angle. Glue in any items for extra security if so desired.

*Pretty fabric bows in harmonizing shades of
pink add a special note for a wedding, dance, or
other festive occasion.*

SEASHORE MEMORABILIA

REMINISCENT OF long idyllic days at the beach, the soothing hues of the clematis, wild poppy seed heads, starfish, and shells are enhanced by the darker tones of the twisted olive wreath.

You will need:

2 sprays clematis, approximately 6 flowers

olive or grapevine wreath

10–15 large poppy seed heads

10–15 beach-collected shells

7–10 starfish

1 spray of dogwood or about 5 other small round flowers

wire or strong twine

heavy gauge wires

spray paint

glue or glue gun

1 Make a loop for hanging with either wire or strong twine. Cut the clematis and leaves off the main stem. Insert these into the wreath by threading the stems through the grapevine or by gluing directly onto the wreath. They should be placed centrally on the wreath or angled slightly in, not out.

2 Cut the stems of the poppy seed heads short and glue them onto the wreath. Take some around to the sides of the wreath. Spray some of the shells blue, following the instructions on the cannister. Glue a length of wire to each shell and thread these through the wreath, adding extra glue if necessary.

3 Glue the wires at right angles to the undersurface of the starfish. Insert these into the wreath at pleasing intervals. Add the dogwood cut into short sprays. (Note: For conservation reasons, try to buy artificial starfish.)

ENCHANTED CIRCLE

A MELLOW mix of fruits, flowers, and moss is captured in an intertwined circlet of contorted willow. The warm tones are reminiscent of late summer warmth and fruitfulness.

You will need:

paper ribbon, about 42 inches in length

round foam ring about 10 inches diameter

heavy gauge wires (or 30–40 moss pins)

5 round artificial fruits, such as apples or plums

glue

3 golden mushrooms

2 large handfuls of reindeer moss

5–7 dry-look roses or other round flowers

6 dried orange slices

2 stems of mini poinsettias or any other spray flower

1–2 stems fresh contorted willow

1 Untwist the paper ribbon with damp hands. Weave it loosely back and forth around the ring. Keep the ribbon in place with lengths of wire bent into hairpins or with moss pins. Place the fruits at regular intervals around the ring, angled up or in but not out. If there are no stems, glue them directly onto the foam, or glue wire onto the fruit.

2 Sharpen the stem ends of the golden mushrooms to a point, or attach to false stems and insert at regular intervals around the ring.

3 Cover most of the bare areas with moss, paying particular attention to the inner and outer extremities. Tease out the moss to give a light covering. Attach with pins.

44

4 Cut the stem of the roses, or other round flowers, and insert at intervals (individually or grouped) around the ring.

5 Wire the orange slices together in twos. Take a wire through the slices, close to the pith. Twist tightly and cut the wire ends to a suitable length. Insert at regular intervals.

6 Cut the poinsettias into smaller sprays. Insert the ends so that the flowers and leaves fall loosely over the other components.

7 Cut the contorted willow into shorter lengths. Tuck one end into the foam and cross the stem over or across the ring. Repeat until your twigs all intertwine.

SUMMER REFLECTIONS

A JOYOUS grouping of late summer roses, plums, and grapevine entwined around a reflecting glass. The strong form of the plums rhythmically leads the eye around the design. The restrained color harmony of the deep burgundy roses and plums is enlivened by the two-toned hydrangeas and the vibrant green of the grapevine.

You will need:

a length of ribbon or picture wire	moss pins
strong glue	
a mirror surrounded by strong floral foam. Alternatively, glue a dry foam ring onto a round mirror glass	3–5 large roses about the same size as the plums

a spray holding 5 plums or other round fruits	5–9 golden mushrooms

a spray, or part of a garland, of grapevine or any foliage with roundish leaves	1 large hydrangea
2 large handfuls of reindeer moss	
	spray roses or other small round flowers

1 Place the ribbon or picture wire across the back of the mirror. Secure in place on either side with a moss pin reinforced by a good drop of glue.

2 Cut the plums off the main stem, keeping any leaves for covering the foam at a later stage. Place the plums at more or less regular intervals around the mirror, angling them upright or slightly inward.

3 Cut off short lengths of grapevine and insert the stems into the foam. Distribute the large roses around the ring.

4 Cover some of the inner and outer areas with moss. Secure this in place with moss pins. More moss can be added later.

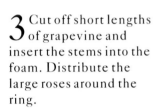

5 Place the golden mushrooms at intervals around the mirror. Break the hydrangea head into smaller flowerets. Take a light wire through the secondary stems, bring down, and twist to form a stem.

6 Fill in with spray roses, moss, or leaves. Keep the larger, more dominant components away from the outer edge or the eye will be led out of the design.

AUTUMNAL SWAG

LADEN WITH fruits, flowers, nuts, and berries, an autumnal swag can be hung on the wall or used to decorate the Thanksgiving table. Designed in rich warm tones of orange, brown, and terracotta, it will remain a welcoming feature throughout the year.

You will need:

a block of foam

a length of carpet gripper, approximately 22 inches long

florist's tape

approximately 2 yards wide wired ribbon

moss pins

1 spray of large plums, or other round fruits

1 large pick of chrysanthemums with foliage and 7–9 small sprays

3–7 lotus seed heads

5–7 golden mushrooms

2 sprays of filberts

1 large spray of blackberries or several smaller ones

1–2 sprays of dogwood

extra foliage if needed

a length of solid material, 22 inches long and 3 inches wide, with the raw edges turned under

1 Cut the block of foam lengthwise into 4 rectangular pieces, and impale on the gripper. (If hanging the swag, first drill a hole at one end of the gripper and position the foam so that it stops short of the hole.) For additional support, wrap foam with florist's tape.

2 Attach the ribbon to the foam with moss pins. Start at the top and work very loosely from side to side, leaving plenty of space between the ribbon and the foam. Reserve approximately ¾ yard for the bow. Cut the plums off the main stem and place in a sinuous curve within the design, not too close to the top and bottom.

3 Dot the larger chrysanthemums through the design. You can repeat the flowing curve, but looser than that created with the plums. Wire the lotus seed heads (see page 26) and insert in the foam.

48

4 Insert the golden
mushrooms. If they
do not have a stem, glue
a short length of wire to
the base (see page 27).
Cut small sprays of
filberts and add through
the design. Add the
blackberries in small
clusters and the sprays of
small chrysanthemums.
Place individual dogwood
flowers at intervals. The
lighter color will lift the
others and give the design
vitality. Fill in with extra
foliage.

5 Make a bow (see page
27). Insert the wire
ends into the top of the
foam. Run glue down the
back of the carpet gripper
and attach the fabric
backing.

BASKETS

WHETHER RUSTIC *or elegant, baskets*
complement the textures and colors of
artificial flowers to perfection. Possible styles
range from a rural basket of spring flowers to
a classic table arrangement of white peonies.
All kinds of baskets can be pressed into service
or you can make your own out of twigs or
branches. You can even spray-paint them
different colors if desired. Moss is useful for
hiding foam or for filling in gaps.

TWIGGY BASKET

NEAT CLUSTERS of roses nestling in small twiggy baskets bound with a natural twine create an unusual and attractively rustic effect.

You will need:

a small plastic pot, about 2½ inches in diameter

adhesive parcel tape

a piece of foam

glue or glue gun

30–50 reasonably straight twigs, a little longer than the height of the pot

roll of natural twine

1–2 sprays of rose foliage

about 12 small roses

1 Cover the plastic pot with parcel tape. This will allow the twigs to adhere to the pot more securely. Cut foam to size and wedge it into the pot so that it rises to just below the rim.

2 Glue the twigs to the side of the pot. They should be even at the base but uneven at the top.

3 Secure and decorate with twine tied with a bow.

4 Cut the sprays of foliage into smaller pieces. If you have leaves with a stem too weak to be inserted, create a false stem (see page 25). Insert the foliage sprays into the foam to cover.

5 Dot the roses through the foliage to complete.

CLASSIC PEONIES

A MASS OF glorious white peonies tumble from a white wire basket, recalling the famous Dutch and French flower paintings of the 18th century. It makes a beautifully cool summer display.

You will need:

frogs and floral clay

a metal basket with inner container, or a large oval basket without handles

a block of foam

3 large picks of peonies or other round flowers such as hydrangeas or garden roses. You will need a mixture of approximately 30 flowers and buds with their foliage

1 Place a length of floral clay around the base of each frog. Secure these to the base of the container.

2 Place a piece of foam on the frogs. The foam should not rise as high as the rim of the container.

3 Cut the secondary stems off the peony picks. Leave as long a stem as possible. They can be shortened later if necessary.

4 Place a stem of foliage (with or without a bud) approximately the same height or slightly taller than the container, centrally in the foam. Angle other stems from this central area over the rim.

5 Continue building up the framework with the foliage and buds. Each stem should appear to radiate from the central area.

6 Start to fill in with larger flowers within the framework already established.

7 Continue to add flowers until the volume of flowers is approximately one and a half times that of the container.

Using one type and color of flower for an arrangement is a slightly unusual but bold move. The foliage acts as a foil for the flowers, and the container harmonizes with the color scheme while adding a textural note. The result is a classically simple yet striking arrangement.

$\mathscr{M}$EADOW $\mathscr{F}$LOWERS

A RIOTOUS mixture of red poppies, blue bachelor's buttons, and white margarita daisies is combined with wheat, foliage, and grasses in a rustic basket.

You will need:

1 large frog (or 2 small ones) and floral clay, or a long heavy wire

a large basket

a piece of foam

sprays of oak or other foliage

12–20 stems of wheat

6–8 sprays of poppies

6–8 sprays of bachelor's buttons

6–8 sprays of margarita daisies

7–10 sprays of bear grass

1 Wind a coil of floral clay around the base of the frog and place it in the basket. Place a piece of foam on the frog. This should fill about one third of the area inside the basket. If there are gaps in the basket weave, try an alternative method of securing the foam. Push a U-shaped piece of heavy wire through the gaps up into the foam. Bend the protruding wire ends back into the foam. Create a framework with the oak, radiating each stem from the central area of the foam.

2 Reinforce the shape created with the oak by adding the stems of wheat.

3 Place the poppies through the design. Cut the stems if necessary to give shorter, lighter sprays. Add the bachelor's buttons, again cutting the stems down into smaller sprays where necessary.

4 Introduce the daisies, placing them through the design. Remember to radiate the stems from the central area.

5 Finally add the sprays of bear grass (shortening the stems if necessary) to give gentle movement throughout the design.

COMPLEMENTARY HARMONIES

THE PURPLE pansies and vibrant yellow chrysanthemums create a dazzling color scheme. It has been set in a simple log basket and decorated with a frothy organdy bow.

You will need:

basket

inner container

frog and floral clay

a block of foam

wire

a garland, large pick, or several sprays of cream and green variegated foliage

2–3 stems spray pansies

2 sprays of chrysanthemums or sunflowers

a generous yard of organdy ribbon

1 If your basket has an uneven base, insert an inner container. This can be a cookie sheet or seed tray (anything that fits the basket). Secure the frog to the tray with floral clay.

2 Cut a piece of foam to fill approximately half the container. Cut off the corners to create a larger surface area and impale the foam on the frog.

3 Insert short sprays of foliage, all radiating from the central area. Bring some of the leaves down over the rim of the basket.

4 Cut the sprays of pansies into shorter lengths. Dot the pansies through the arrangement.

5 Create a bow with the organdy ribbon (see page 27), and insert the wire stem into the foam, off center.

6 Cut the yellow flowers off the stems and add these to the arrangement.

BEAUTIFUL BASKET

THIS ATTRACTIVE design can be created in minutes to provide the perfect container for potpourri, fruit, nuts, or a special gift.

You will need:

a basket

4 sprays of roses in two closely harmonizing colors

a few extra leaves and smaller flowers

glue gun or strong glue

1 Cut the roses and leaves off the main stems, leaving only a stub of a stem on the flowers.

2 Position the principal flowers around the basket in a pleasing combination of color and size, taking care to angle some of the flowers over the rim of the basket.

3 When you are satisfied with their arrangement, glue them in place. The slim stems of the leaves can be glued and slotted under the flowers.

4 Fill in with smaller flowers and extra foliage if necessary. If the flowers are much smaller, group them in twos or threes to maintain the scale.

VASES

VASES COME *in a huge range of colors, shapes, and textures; the choice is almost overwhelming. Initially, choose one or two classic shapes and colors; then as your confidence grows, experiment with more unusual materials and designs. The key points to remember are that the size of the vase must be in proportion to the flowers used, the container should complement rather than dominate the arrangement, and there should be a color link between the container and the flowers.*

GOURDS AND TULIPS

A CLEAR GLASS vase contains an assortment of smooth, colorful gourds and is topped by a crescent of exuberantly feathered tulips, lotus seed heads, and rough-textured sponge mushrooms.

You will need:

large glass vase with a narrow opening

5–7 artificial or dried gourds

candlecup or small dish to fit steadily in the opening when secured with floral clay

cylinder or piece of foam

frog and floral clay

about 10 feathered tulips in two coordinating colors

2–3 sponge mushrooms

wire

glue gun or strong glue

5–7 large lotus seed heads, sprayed gold

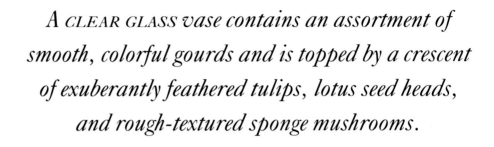

1 Place the gourds so that they fill approximately half the vase. Secure the candlecup or dish to the top of the container with floral clay. Cut foam and secure with frog and clay.

2 Create a bold block of color with the more strongly colored tulips. Position this block slightly off center.

3 Attach wire stems to the sponge mushrooms (see page 27) and attach them to the side of the foam, so that they curve down over the top third of the vase.

4 Cut leaves off some of the tulips and attach the long tulip leaves to the opposite side of the foam, building up a crescent-shaped design.

5 Add the second color of tulips. Fill in at the side and the back to make a smooth shape. Wire the lotus seed heads (see page 26) and use them to fill the uncovered area and complete the bold crescent design.

BLUE HARVEST CLUSTER

ANEMONES, REPEATING the deep blue of the container, nestle alongside pears and berries in a neat "blocked" design that is easy to make and delightful to view.

You will need:

frog and floral clay

blue pottery container

a piece of foam

5–6 pears on picks or with wire stems

7–10 anemones

3–4 picks of berries

1 Put a coil of floral clay on the base of the frog and place on the bottom of the container.

2 Cut a piece of foam to fill most of the container, but stop just short of the rim.

3 Make one grouping of pears, so that they seem to rise from the central area of the foam. Leave as little space as possible between them. If they do not have stems, glue a short piece of wire to each.

4 Block the anemones, one by one, next to the pears.

5 Fill the remaining third with the berry picks to provide a dense area of berries and foliage. There should be no space between the three components in this compact design.

$\mathcal{S}$UMMER $\mathcal{B}$LUES

A FLOWING *exuberance of delphiniums, agapanthus, clematis, and scabious gives a soothing design for the hottest of summer days.*

You will need:

2-inch gauge chicken wire. It should be approximately 2½ times the depth of the container opening and a little wider than the width of the opening

gray urn or container

sand

10–15 sprays of foliage such as eucalyptus, rose leaf, or ivy

round flowers such as agapanthus, hydrangea, and peonies

line flowers such as delphiniums and larkspur

spray flowers such as clematis and scabious

hosta leaves (optional)

1 Cut a piece of chicken wire to size and cut off the selvage. Scrunch up the wire, keeping the loose ends on top and away from your hands (see page 26).

2 Insert the wire into the urn, allowing some of the loose ends to protrude. These can be wrapped around individual stems to give extra support. Add sand through the wire to give further support.

3 Place a stem of foliage to establish the height. It should be central, about two-thirds of the way back, and approximately the same height as the urn.

4 Insert two further sprays of foliage, one at each side of the container, so that the three sprays together give a loose triangular shape.

5 Fill in the three-dimensional form of the arrangement, following the shape established in step 4. Bring shorter sprays down over the rim of the container at the front and back.

6 Reinforce the foliage framework with line flowers. Radiate all stems from the central area.

7 Position your round flowers within the arrangement. Avoid placing them too close to the outer margins.

8 Start to add the spray flowers, filling out the design. Add more round, line, or spray flowers or foliage as required.

This is a very traditional arrangement with its balanced mixture of flower forms, cool, harmonious colors, and classic container.

$\mathscr{V}$ICTORIANA

_____ _____

A MASS of dry-look roses, peonies, and hydrangeas is arranged simply with aspidistra leaves in a handsome red-glazed pot.

a large round container

dry foam

florists' tape

frog and floral clay

7–10 large, single leaves such as aspidistra or hosta. These could be from a house plant

5–7 dry-look, teal blue hydrangeas

7–9 dry-look, cream open roses

5–7 dry-look, red spray peonies

3–5 dry-look, cream and burgundy roses

3–5 sprays of burgundy plums on stems, or any other round fruit

1 Place foam in the container to fill approximately two-thirds of the interior. It should be level with the rim of the container and secured with frog and floral clay. Take florists' tape across the foam for added security. Create a framework with the aspidistra leaves. The final arrangement should be a tight mass of plant material about one and a half times the volume of the container. Radiate all stems from the central area and angle some of the leaves down over the rim of the container.

2 Place the hydrangeas and then the cream roses, continuing to radiate the stems.

3 Add the peonies. It may be necessary to cut these into smaller sprays. Angle one or two gently over the rim. Dot in the cream and burgundy roses. Fill in the design with the plums and any other round flowers and fruit you have on hand. There should be little or no space between the different elements of the design.

CINNAMON VARIATIONS

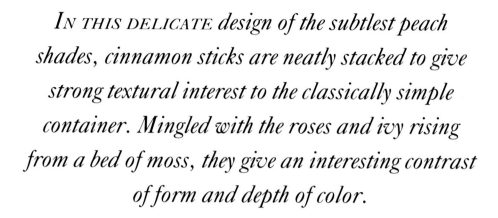

You will need:

square glass vase

frog and floral clay

a block of foam

moss to cover

moss pins or wire hairpins

40–50 short cinnamon sticks

1 spray of ivy or other small round-leaved foliage

10–12 roses or other round flowers

1–2 stems of small spray flowers

wires to extend cinnamon sticks

IN THIS DELICATE design of the subtlest peach shades, cinnamon sticks are neatly stacked to give strong textural interest to the classically simple container. Mingled with the roses and ivy rising from a bed of moss, they give an interesting contrast of form and depth of color.

1 Place the frog and floral clay on the base of the glass vase. Cut a piece of foam slightly taller but the same shape as the container.

2 Leave just enough space for the cinnamon sticks to be stacked between the foam and the glass on each side. Cut the cinnamon sticks (with scissors or a serrated knife) to fit the space between the foam and the container. Leave about 10 sticks for step 6.

3 Spread reindeer moss over the foam and secure with pins.

4 Cut a length of the ivy spray approximately the height of the container and place centrally. Cut other sprays, approximately the same length, and place them so that they radiate from the center. Bend some of the stems so that they are angled over the rim of the container.

5 Add the roses, keeping within the outline of the foliage. Continue to radiate every stem from the central area.

6 Cut the stem(s) of spray flowers into smaller lengths and use to fill out the design. Wire each cinnamon stick (see page 26) and insert them into the foam, ensuring that the wire is hidden.

SUNFLOWERS

AN ARRAY of bright sunflowers in an old Provençal pot creates a simple but stylish design full of warmth and sunshine.

You will need:

a large earthenware, terracotta, or stoneware pot with a strong form

sand

clear adhesive tape

about 17–20 sunflowers

a handful of moss

1 Pour sand into the vase to help keep the stems in place. Then take lengths of narrow adhesive tape from one side of the rim to the other, making a grid with enough space for the sunflower stems to be inserted.

2 Place the first stem through the central part of the grid and down into the sand. If necessary, extend the length of the stems (see page 25). Add more flowers, positioning them at different angles to give more interest.

3 Cover the tape grid with a little moss if it still shows when you have positioned all the stems.

COPPER REFLECTIONS

An INFORMAL *mix of oranges, pinks, and blues is enhanced by the burnished copper of the pitcher.*

You will need:

dry foam

a copper pitcher or container

7–9 sprays of foliage

12–15 mixed sweet peas or other line flowers

3–5 sprays of deep blue asters

9–11 orange roses

other round flowers in harmonious colors

3–5 sprays of Himalayan poppies (*Meconopsis*)

1 Carve the foam into a cork shape to fit the pitcher. Firmly wedge the foam so that it rises above the rim. Create a framework with the foliage. Place the first stem centrally toward the back, approximately the same height as the container plus foam. Insert two slightly shorter stems in each side of the foam, angled downward. Add more stems to complete the framework and make a loosely triangular shape. Angle two short sprays over the front rim. All stems should radiate from the central area.

2 Reinforce the shape with sweetpeas or line flowers. Give depth to the design by placing material through the central area. Add the sprays of asters (cut into shorter sprays if necessary).

3 Add the roses and other round flowers, taking care to place the larger and stronger colored flowers in the central area. Fill in with the Himalayan poppies and any other material you feel appropriate. Cut the sprays into more manageable lengths if necessary.

OTHER CONTAINERS

BECAUSE YOUR containers do not have to be waterproof, the silk flower arranger has far greater freedom to be innovative than the fresh flower arranger. Arrangements can be placed in terracotta pots, trays, crates, bowls, and metal pitchers, or even left without a container at all, as long as the foam has been concealed. Keep an eye out for unusual containers in secondhand stores or at sales.

FOUNTAIN OF FLOWERS

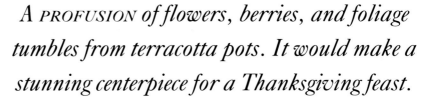

A PROFUSION of flowers, berries, and foliage tumbles from terracotta pots. It would make a stunning centerpiece for a Thanksgiving feast.

You will need:

2 terracotta pots, one a size larger than the other

frog and floral clay

foam to fit the pots

handful of moss

moss pins

florists' tape

large pick or several sprays of ranunculuses with foliage

7–9 mini terracotta pots

beans and legumes

glue gun or strong glue

7–9 heavy gauge wires

several sprays or 1 large pick of chrysanthemums with foliage

about 3 sprays of nasturtiums

5–7 picks of berries

vine foliage and grapes

1 Wedge foam into the two pots so that it rises about 2 inches above the rims. Lightly cover the foam in the smaller pot with moss and secure with moss pins. Place a frog and clay underneath the smaller pot. Insert its prongs into the foam of the larger pot.

2 Lightly cover any exposed foam in the larger pot with moss. Take florists' tape over and down the sides of the two pots if extra security is desired. Cut the ranunculuses and their foliage into smaller sprays. Use the foliage and buds to create a rough framework. Allow some of the plant material to flow down over the rims of the two pots.

3 Place a strip of glue inside the mini pots. Pat on a selection of beans and legumes, taking care not to burn yourself if using a gun. Repeat, to achieve a denser covering. Glue a heavy gauge wire outside each pot on the same side as the legumes. Or, insert wire through hole and twist the short end around the long end. Place the pots through the design.

4 Split up the sprays or picks of chrysanthemums and add these to fill out the design. Cut the nasturtiums into shorter lengths and add these, allowing them to flow down over the rims.

5 Add the berries and grapes. Glue firmly in place. Fill in with vine leaves and other foliage to give an impression of autumnal abundance.

*W*INTER *C*HEER

*S*ILK *FLOWERS* *and thistles are mixed with fragrant fresh blue spruce, other long-lasting foliage, and dried artichokes to provide a dramatic focal point throughout the festive season.*

You will need:

wet foam

long plastic trays to fit the length of the mantelpiece

florists' tape

5 thick candles, only the two short ones need to be the same size

wooden skewers

3 large sprays of blue spruce

long-lasting evergreen foliage such as ivy, laurel, conifer, skimmia

7–10 arum lilies

3 large dried artichokes

4–6 large thistles or cardoons

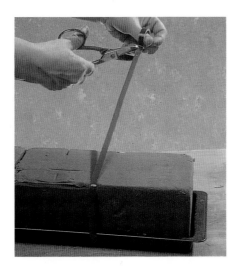

1 Allow the wet foam blocks to sink beneath their own weight in water. This should take about 90 seconds. Then fill the trays with foam and wrap florists' tape securely around at regular intervals. Place the trays in position. If necessary, leave gaps between the trays to fit the length exactly.

2 Secure the wooden skewers to the candles using florists' tape. Make a grouping of three candles in the center and one short candle toward each end. To give a candle extra height, use longer lengths of stick and allow the candle to stand above the foam.

3 Create a framework with short lengths of blue spruce. Place the first stem upright behind the central placement of candles. This will be the highest point of the design and all other stems should appear to radiate from this area. Place the next two stems, one out of each end, so that they sweep down over the sides of the mantelpiece. Work so that the remaining stems of spruce fill in the crescent-shaped outline created by the first three stems.

4 Reinforce the spruce framework with conifer or other foliage.

5 Place the arum lilies through the design, radiating (or appearing to radiate) the stems from the central area and keeping within the framework already established.

6 Group the three dried artichokes loosely around the center of the arrangement. Radiate the thistles through the design.

7 Add the skimmia, ivy, and other foliage to make a full, luxuriant design still within the original framework.

The fireplace is always the focal point of a room, and this pleasing arrangement of foliage, flowers, and candles will ensure that the mantelpiece is worthy of attention.

ℰXOTIC 𝒜NTHURIUMS

THE STRONG forms of the white anthuriums stand out boldly against the deep green of the tropical foliage. The clean, cool colors are reflected in the heavy chunks of glass.

1 Place the foam on the lead frog. Insert the pick of leaves centrally.

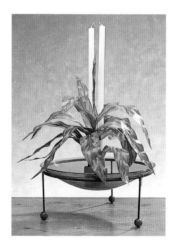

2 Place one of the candles in a candleholder. If it is too loose, place a thin coil of floral clay around the candle before insertion. Attach short lengths of wire or toothpicks with tape around the base of the second candle. Insert both candles in the central area. One candle will be slightly higher than the other.

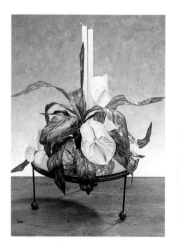

3 Place the three anthuriums at different heights, each at a different angle. Place the glass chunks so that they hide the uncovered mechanics.

PEDESTAL OF FLOWERS

COMBINE A *single type of foliage with a wealth of different flowers, and you will have a cohesive design with panache. Add an up-to-the-minute container in wrought iron and glass, and you will have a modern design with a timeless feel.*

You will need:

a wrought iron pedestal with a glass bowl

a block of foam

large plastic frog and floral clay

40–50 stems of silk, fresh, or dried eucalyptus. Eucalyptus will dry *in situ* if placed in dry foam

a mix of large-scale round flowers, such as roses, peonies, and hydrangeas

a mix of line flowers such as snapdragons and foxgloves

a mix of spray flowers such as spray roses and dogwood

1 Place the large frog and floral clay in the base of the glass bowl and impale the block of foam on it. Establish the height of the arrangement with a stem of eucalyptus placed centrally in the foam.

2 Surround the foam with the stems of eucalyptus in order to hide it and give a single foil to the host of different flowers you will be using. Radiate several stems out of the top of the foam to fill in the framework.

3 Add the line flowers to reinforce the shape you have created. If areas of foam still show, moss can be added.

4 Add the round flowers. Fill in with spray flowers. Continue to add any other flowers you have available or further stems of eucalyptus.

*A pedestal
arrangement is
independent of any
furniture and can
stand in a corner, be
made the focus of
attention in a
hallway, or placed at
the end of a passage.*

CHRISTMAS LIGHTS

COMBINE CABBAGES with blue spruce, poinsettias, and candles to create a traditional Christmas arrangement with a difference.

two 12-inch candles

toothpicks and florists' tape

about 10 short sprays of blue spruce

2 latex cabbages

2 lengths of quality wired ribbon, each about 1 yard long

2 medium gauge wires

2 poinsettias

1 Anchor a frog in the base of the dish. Place a piece of foam on it and chamfer the sides. Attach four toothpicks to a piece of florists' tape. Wrap the tape around the bottom of each candle. Insert the toothpicks in the foam so that the two candles stand at varying heights. Make sure that both are stable.

2 Radiate sprays of blue spruce from the central area of the foam. To make the oval shape, place longer sprays at opposite ends and two shorter pieces on each side.

3 Radiate short sprays of spruce out from the top of the foam to make the spruce outline three-dimensional.

4 On both sides of the arrangement, insert a cabbage. Check that the design is actually, and visually, well balanced.

5 Find the central point of one of the lengths of ribbon. Cross the ends over the central point to form two loops. Wrap a wire tightly around the point where the loops cross and twist, leaving two long wires for insertion in the foam. Repeat for the second.

6 Insert the bows in the spaces between the cabbages.

7 Remove any foliage from the poinsettias and insert them in the spaces. If the arrangement appears heavy, create better proportions by substituting taller candles.

RISING HIGH

An ECLECTIC mix of foliage is positioned to provide a leafy framework for the simple purity of a few open roses. It makes a luxuriant foundation for the elegance of the candles.

You will need:

frog and floral clay

shallow glass bowl

piece of foam

toothpicks and florists' tape

2 tall candles 12–15 inches high

candle holder

all the spare leaves that you have been told never to throw away! You should try and use good contrasts of form and texture

about 7 round flowers, of a strong hue

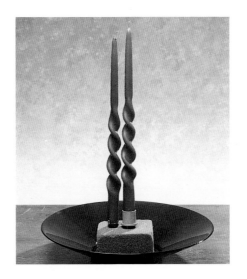

1 Place the floral clay on the base of the frog and attach it to the center of the bowl. Attach a piece of foam that is the approximate size of the base, but does not rise as high as the rim of the bowl. Use the toothpicks-and-tape method (see page 27) to attach one of the candles to the center of the foam. Place the second one in the candleholder so that the candles are at different heights.

2 Place the foliage stems in the foam. Angle them so that the foliage creates a low mound, filling the well of the bowl.

3 Continue to add foliage, taking care to cover the foam. Ensure there is a good mix of form and texture. A few variegated leaves will add interest.

4 Cut the flowers short and insert at intervals through the foliage.

5 Continue to add flowers and foliage until there is a pleasing mix.

CRATE OF FRUIT

RIPE FRUIT and dry-look flowers, lined neatly side by side, are cushioned in a soft bed of tillandsia moss. This simple display gives a delightful impression of rural abundance.

You will need:

a small wooden crate

a block of foam

2 or 3 different fruits, enough to complete three widths of the crate

about 2 thick cinnamon sticks

enough dry-look roses, or any full round flower, to complete two widths of the crate

a large handful of tillandsia moss

1 Cut the foam to fit the crate snugly but stop short of the rim.

2 Position the fruit in lines along the short side of the crate. If you are using stemless fruits, glue a short wire to the base of the fruit (see page 27) or glue directly onto the foam. Cut cinnamon sticks into short lengths with a serrated knife. Place them upright in a line along the central row of fruit.

3 Fill in with rows of dry-look roses. Pack them close together to give an impression of abundance.

4 Tuck the moss between the fruit and flowers to hide the foam. Complete by tucking moss between the slats of the crate.

$\mathscr{S}$WEET AND $\mathscr{S}$IMPLE

POSITION A few daisies or rudbeckias around a chunky beeswax candle, and you will have a table arrangement that will give pleasure and light the whole year round.

You will need:

frog and floral foam

cylinder or piece of foam

a small round dish

sandpaper

2–3 heavy gauge wires

large chunky beeswax candle

a decorative outer container (optional)

10–14 round leaves such as ivy or vine

about 30 round flowers such as rudbeckias or daisies. These can be cut from sprays or a pick

1 Coil the floral clay around the base of the frog and attach it to the base of the small dish. If you are using foam cut from a block, cut a piece a little larger than the base of the candle. Create a cylinder the same circumference as the candle by sandpapering away the edges. Cut the wire into five equal lengths. Heat the ends with a match or over a flame, and slide them smoothly into the base of the candle.

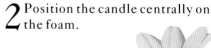

2 Position the candle centrally on the foam.

3 If desired, place the plastic dish in a more attractive outer container. Make a ring of foliage just above the rim of the container.

4 Cut the flowers from the sprays with short stems.

5 Make two rings of flowers between the candle and the leaves. Position the second ring of flowers so that they are not lined up directly above the first layer.

FLOWERS TO WEAR

SILK FLOWERS *are ideal for weddings – your chosen blooms can be out of season and any color you like; they will look their best regardless of the weather or careless handling; and above all, they will be a lasting memento of the day. Hats for weddings, or other special occasions, take on a touch of designer class with the addition of one or two pure silk flowers, which can be changed to suit any outfit.*

MILLINERY SPLENDOR

Take a fine straw hat, a soft piece of voile, and two silk flowers and with them produce a creation worthy of a designer label. The principles can be adapted to any style for any occasion.

You will need:

a fine straw hat

a length of voile long enough to fit round the brim of the hat and about 3 times the required width

needle and heavy thread to match the hat

2 pure silk flowers

1 Slipstich along the raw edges of the two short sides of a piece of voile and loosely gather in each side.

2 Fold the long sides in to give several layers. Place this around the brim of the hat. Using a sharp needle and double thread, secure the material to the hat, first at several points on the seam and then make a couple of stitches at various points around the brim.

3 Pin the flowers on the hat, ensuring they are attractively positioned. Push the needle and thread through the stems in one or two places. Do this several times to secure them. If your flowers do not have stems, stitch a couple of back petals onto the hat.

4 Adjust the leaves to cover some of the stems and to enhance the flowers. Because stitching has been used rather than glue, other flowers can easily be substituted, perhaps to match another outfit, without spoiling the hat.

$\mathscr{F}$LOWER GIRL'S $\mathscr{B}$ASKET

*E*ARLY *S*PRING *flowers, carefully chosen for compatibility of scale and season, are harmoniously mixed in a small posy basket. The choice of flowers can be adapted to suit any season and outfit.*

You will need:

small posy basket, in scale with the height of the flower girl

small piece of foam

small handful of moss

moss pins

1–2 ivy sprays, or other small-scale foliage

5 small sprays of winter aconites

5–8 sprays of snowdrops

5–7 crocus

5 small sprays of sweet violets

5–7 sprays of violas

2 lengths of ribbon, each about a yard long, in coordinating colors

1 Wedge the foam into the basket. Place a light covering of moss over the foam. Secure with moss pins.

2 Radiate small sprays of foliage from the central area of the foam. Avoid obscuring the handle.

3 Place the winter aconites through the basket. Add the snowdrops.

4 Insert the crocus, continuing to radiate the stems from the central area. Add the sweet violets.

5 Add the violas, cutting down the stems into shorter sprays where necessary. When you are satisfied with the arrangement, you may wish to glue all the stem ends in place in the foam, for security.

6 Tie the two lengths of ribbon around the base of the handle. Cut the trailing ends to a suitable length for the flower girl.

$\mathcal{P}$EACHES AND $\mathcal{C}$REAM

AN EVERLASTING memento of a special day – pure silk roses are the centerpiece for a sumptuous confection in peaches and cream.

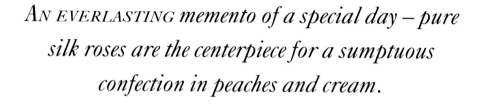

You will need:

a bridal bouquet holder containing dry foam

a length of cord or ribbon

glue gun or strong glue

3–4 sprays of ivy, either plain, variegated, or a mixture of both

about 5 large oval leaves

5 large round silk flowers such as roses

a mixture of round, line, and spray silk flowers, complementary in size and color

1 Wrap the cord or ribbon around the handle of the bouquet holder and glue firmly in place. As a general guide, the finished length of the bouquet should be about one third of the bride's height.

2 Create the framework of the bouquet with sprays of ivy. Curve a long length downward. Add a second stem, about half the length of the first, curving gently toward the bride. Take two more stems, the same length as the second

one. Place these at right angles to the first two stems to form a cross. To create the third dimension, insert a short central stem, following the line of the handle. All stems should appear to radiate from the center.

3 Fill in the bouquet, keeping within the framework established in step 2. It will be viewed from the sides as well as the front, so ensure that the stems curve naturally over the sides to hide the rim of the holder.

4 Add the larger leaves. Place them carefully to give an uncontrived look. Their smooth texture will be an attractive foil to the flowers.

5 Add line flowers. They should reinforce the framework of the bouquet. All stems must radiate from the center. Add round focal flowers. Position the first toward the bride. Take a line of these flowers through the bouquet, crossing the central area about one third of the way down, close to the central stem. Place the flowers at different angles.

6 Fill in the design with a variety of flowers to give a good contrast of form, color and texture. When you are satisfied with the overall design, glue flowers and foliage permanently into position. The back should be neat so that there is no risk of damage to the bride's outfit.

BRIDAL CORSAGE

A CLOUD *of rose petals creates a romantic corsage for the bride or members of the bridal party.*

You will need:

a short length of a light gauge wire, covered with stem tape

stem tape

2 tight buds (optional)

3 open buds

5 single rose leaves on a short light stem

1 full open rose

a clip or pin

1 Position the base of a leaf parallel with the tip of the wire and stem tape the two together. If the stems of the flowers you are using are thick and bulky, add lighter wires and cover with stem tape.

2 Bind the first tight bud onto the wire, angled to one side. Add the first open bud to the opposite side. The second placement should be slightly lower. Do not stem tape right up to the base of each flower to allow for flexibility.

3 Place a leaf behind the open bud. Tape in the second open bud and then the third, with a further leaf behind. Move slightly down the light gauge wire as you add each placement.

4 Position the open rose centrally and stem tape in. Add another leaf. All the stems should lie parallel.

5 Add the remaining leaves and trim the wire ends. Fix the clip to the back of the corsage, close to the central point of gravity and stem tape in. A small piece of floral clay can be used to ensure that the head of the clip is in close contact with the central stem. Alternatively, insert a corsage pin at a right angle through the stem.

TOPIARY

TOPIARY CAN *be very formal – cones of fruit
and vegetables and intricately pruned trees –
or exuberant – vines entwined around arches
and up obelisks. Floral foam can be
purchased in spherical or conical shapes,
which makes formal arrangements much
easier. Informal topiary has few rules and
you can give your imagination free rein – the
examples in this section could not be more
different in style and approach.*

BYZANTINE CONE

A CLASSICAL urn holds a cone of fruits in the spirit of the Byzantine period. This formal mass of fruits and leaves forms a symmetrical spire rich in texture and color, giving an elegant and dignified design.

You will need:

a block of foam

an urn or other symmetrically shaped container, with an opening a little larger than the circumference of the cone

a straight twig

a dry foam cone, or alternatively carve a block of foam to shape

wire

glue

selection of fruits on picks or with wire stems attached. For a 12-inch cone, you will need about 50 pieces of fruit

about 30 leaves

1 Cut the foam to fit the inside of the container and wedge it firmly inside.

2 Insert one end of the twig in the center of the foam, and impale the cone to secure it in place. Use lengths of wire bent into hairpins to give extra security.

3 If the fruits are not on a pick, glue a short wire to the base of each one. Insert the fruits into the cone until it is covered. Dot the fruits around the cone, or work section by section. Position them to create a pleasing and varied effect of form, color, and texture.

4 Tuck the leaves between the fruits.

5 Adjust the fruits where necessary. If the top placement looks awkward, replace with a smaller fruit. Do not be afraid to angle the stems sharply into the foam where necessary.

TOPIARY TREES

REMINISCENT OF *the fruit trees in the Orangerie at Versailles in France, these small clipped topiaries, bearing fruits, seed heads, and flowers, stand proudly upright on their trunks of cinnamon. The subtle hues of the flowers and berries are enhanced by the dark green foliage.*

You will need:

about 4 long cinnamon sticks

rubber band

clear adhesive tape or florist's tape

a plastic plant pot about 2½ inches in diameter

plaster of Paris

dry foam ball

glue

handful of reindeer moss

handful of moss pins

2 stems of rosehips with their leaves

2 stems spray roses or other small flowers, with their leaves

2 stems of spray berries

a few extra small leaves (if necessary)

7–9 mini lotus seed heads (optional)

decorative outer pot

1 Hold the cinnamon sticks so that they are even at the bottom. The one or two longer stems at the top will be enough to hold the ball without making too large a hole in the foam. Hold these together with a rubber band.

2 Place clear adhesive tape or florist's tape over the holes in the plastic pot to prevent the wet plaster of Paris from seeping through.

3 Mix the plaster of Paris quickly and thoroughly with a disposable stick and pour into the pot.

4 Place the cinnamon sticks centrally in the mixture and hold upright for a couple of minutes until the bundle stands unsupported. When the plaster of Paris is completely set, impale the foam ball on the cinnamon sticks. For extra security remove the ball, add some strong glue, and replace.

5 Cover the ball with reindeer moss, using moss pins or wire hairpins to keep it in place.

6 Cut the hips and leaves from the main stem. Place individual leaves or small sprays north, south, east, and west.

7 Place more leaves, on short stems, radiating from the center of the ball so that the entire ball is lightly covered. Dot the rosehips around the ball.

8 Cut or pull the roses and berries off the main stem leaving short stalks. Insert these into the ball at intervals and fill out the sphere with any small leaves you have available. Add seed heads if desired.

9 Place the tree in an attractive outer pot and cover the top with moss. A few berries or seed heads can be added to the moss to give a link with those in the tree itself.

RUSTIC BOWER

TWISTED GRAPEVINE leaves arch gently above wild flowers nestling amid moss-filled terracotta pots. The texture and color of the sack completes the effect of a rural idyll.

You will need:

a sack container. This can be purchased or you can make your own by molding starch-saturated sacking around a suitable sized bowl. (Alternatively, use a container with a piece of burlap wrapped around and taped in place, or a basket without handles.)

inner container

a piece of foam

florist's tape

stem tape

two 12-inch heavy gauge wires

glue

a length of grapevine garland

1 pick of violets or any other suitable flower

two terracotta pots

a handful of moss

1 pick of daisies or dandelions or 7–9 round flowers in scale with the violets

1 Place an inner dish in the sack. Cut the foam to rise slightly above the rim. Slice off the corners of the foam to give a greater working area. Replace the foam in the inner container and secure with florist's tape if necessary.

2 To make the arch, wind stem tape around seven-eighths of the first wire. Attach the second wire by stem-taping the ends of the first and second wires together. Continue taping to make one length. Curve gently to form an arch.

3 Insert the ends of the wire arch into opposite sides of the foam. Add a dab of glue if necessary. Wind the length of grapevine around the arch, attaching each end with glue.

4 Place the violets at the front of the container at a slight forward angle.

5 Block the daisies or dandelions in a neat group.

6 Add the plant pots on their sides. You can place a small amount of moss in the bottoms of the pots for added textural interest. Cover any bare areas with a little moss.

*O*BELISK

IDEAL AS a striking centerpiece for a stylish house or apartment, this wrought iron topiary would also look dramatic decorated with bougainvillea, clematis, roses, or sweet peas.

You will need:

wrought iron obelisk or cone

outer container or pot

bubble wrap or styrofoam chips

2–4 garlands of geraniums or other flowers

moss

1 Place the obelisk in the outer container and pack the inside with bubble wrap or styrofoam chips which will be covered with moss later.

2 Starting at the bottom, twine the geranium garland round the four upright struts of the obelisk.

3 Continue to the top. If feasible, place the smaller flowers and buds near the top and the larger ones toward the bottom for good visual balance.

4 Introduce a second color geranium if so desired. Cover the packing with a layer of moss.

$\mathscr{I}$NDEX

ACKNOWLEDGMENTS

The author would like to give special thanks to her family – David, Charles, Jane; and Cedric and Joan Ward for all their patience and help during the writing of the book.

Quarto would particularly like to thank **Teters Floral Products Inc.** (see address below) for so generously providing a large number of the polyester blend (silk) flowers, and the latex berries and fruit from their Semblance line for use in the book.

Quarto and the author would like to thank the following people and organizations for their assistance in providing materials for this book. While every effort has been made to acknowledge all suppliers, we would like to apologize if any omissions have been made.

ADAM AARONSON, The Old Imperial Laundry, 71 Warriner Gardens, London, SW11 4XW. Tel: 71 627 5555. (Turquoise Fan Vases p.15)

AMAZING GRATES, 61 High Road, London N2 (fireplace pp.88–9)

ANNA FRENCH, 343 Kings Road, London SW3 5ES. For your nearest stockist tel. 71 351 1126. (Wallpapers: Drill Col 056 p.47, Texture Col 040 p.49, p.93 and p.95. Fabrics: Petal Lace p.53, pp.56–7, Empire Madras pp.72–3, Romance Jacquard p.73)

BRIAN YATES INTERIORS Ltd, Riverside Park, Caton Road, Lancaster, LA1 3PE. Tel: 524 35035. London showroom: 26 Chelsea Harbour. Tel: 71 352 0123. (Fabrics: Heversham H19 Strawberry p.85, Heversham H20 Radish p.49 and p.75, Sheila Coombes Spinney Voile 3667–V1 p.85 and pp.93–4)

CROWTHER OF SYON LODGE Ltd, Syon Lodge, Busch Corner, London Road, Islesworth TW7 5BH. Tel: 81 560 7978 (urn p. 6)

DERAN FOLIAGE SUPPLIES, Hanestig, Cilmeri, Pontrhydygroes, Ystrad Meurig, Dyfed SY25 6DJ. Tel: 974 282295 (fresh blue spruce and other foliage pp.86–9)

MATTHEW EDEN, Pickwickend, Corsham, Wiltshire SN13 0JB. Tel: 249 713335 (Obelisk with a hard wood finial and lead container pp.124–5)

JAMES EGGLETON Ltd, 140 High Town Road, Luton, Beds LU2 0DJ (hats pp.106–7 left and center)

EVERBLOOMS Ltd, 53 Romberg Road, Tooting Bec, London SW17 7UB. Tel: 81 767 4942 (anthuriums and other rubber flowers p.11 and pp.90–1)

FLORAL SILK, Unit 29, Kenavon Drive, The Forbury Park, Reading, Berks. Tel: 734 588041 (silk flowers, urn pp.70–3)

JULIANA'S, Unit 4, Lyndon Yard, Riverside Road, London. Tel: 71 937 1555 (rouched ivory silk marquee lining pp.40–1)

KIRKER GREER & Co, 85 High Street, Burnham-on-Crouch, Essex CM00 8AH. Tel: 621 784647 (Beeswax candle pp.102–3)

LELIEVRE U.K. Ltd, 110 Cleveland Street, London W1P 5PN. Tel: 71 636 3461. (Fabric: Eden 5972 02 p.117)

FLOWERS BY NOVELTY IMPORTS Ltd, Michelle House, 45–46 Berners St, London W1P 3AD (pure silk flowers for hats pp.106–7 and corsage pp.104–5)

PETER JONES, Sloane Square, London SW1W 8EL (copper bowls p.81, pecan wood blind p.101)

PONGEES Specialists in Silks, 184–186 Old Street, London EC1V 9FR. Tel: 71 253 0428. (Fabrics: Tussah Silk Range no. 8995/2 pp.4–5, pp.8–9, p.37, pp.114–15, p.123, Indian Doupian 725 no.9 pp.2–3, pp.6–7, p.53 and p.103: no.18 pp.6–7, pp.8–9, p.47, p.63, pp.104–5, p.113, Habotai 504D no.353 p.63)

PRICE'S CANDLE CO. Ltd, 81 Strand, London WC 2R. Tel: 71 379 4329 (candles pp.88–9, pp.90–1)

A I ROOT Co, of Medina, Ohio, USA (candles pp.82–3)

SELFRIDGES Ltd, 400 Oxford St, London W1A. Tel: 71 629 1234. (Sunflower china p.103)

SINO-TRADING COMPANY, Shaw Road, Liverpool L24 9JT (cotton and paper flowers pp.10–11, pp.94–5)

TETERS FLORAL PRODUCTS Inc. 1425 S. Lillian, Bolivar, MO 65613. Tel: 800-999-5996 (majority of silk and latex flowers and fruit)

TRIDENT FOAMS, Marple Road, Offerton, Stockport SK2 5HW. Tel: 61 456 4477 (floral foam, blocks, rings, cones, spheres and Triflora ribbons)

VINCENTS, 51 Somerset Road, London SW19 5HT. Tel: 81 946 4090 (parchment flowers and latex roses p.6, p.11, pp.38–41, pp.94–5)

Violette Gurr at HARWOOD ANTIQUES, 24 Lower Richmond Road, London SW15 1JP. Tel: 81 788 7444 (provencal pots p.79)

WENDY A CUSHING Ltd. Unit M7, Chelsea Garden Market, Chelsea Harbour, London SW10. Tel: 71 351 5796 (thick red and gold cable with red cushion tassels – made to order p.49)

Index by Dorothy Frame